Marble clocks inspired by the Art Nouveau and Art Deco movements are immediately recognisable, as in this example, with a flash of coloured marble, flowing caricatured figures and fiercely angular dial, hands and numerals. Freed from the restraints of a classical tradition, each exhibits a unique, indefinable quality of its own.

MARBLE CLOCKS

Peter Wotton and Brian Oliver

Shire Publications

CONTENTS

ACKNOWLEDGEMENTS
The authors express their grateful thanks to the following for their assistance and permission
to photograph items on their premises: Richard Holmwood of RH Clocks, Tunbridge Wells,
Kent; David Vine-Mood of Trash and Treasure (Clocks), Tunbridge Wells; Shirley and Peter
Lewis of Shirley Antiques, Chatham, Kent. Photography by Peter Wotton.

Cover photograph: *This French marble clock, exuding a powerful sense of presence, has developed a long way from the early, austere Greek-inspired examples. It is ornamented with a modest reference to the Greek column style, deep red marble, gold-filled intaglio, marble and malachite inlay, relief and brass claw feet. The wide and varied use of so much ornamentation is a sure indication that interest in this style of marble clock, from c.1900, was becoming saturated.*

British Library Cataloguing in Publication Data: Wotton, Peter. Marble clocks. – (Shire album; no. 347) 1. Clocks and watches 2. Clocks and watches – History I. Title II. Oliver, Brian 681.1'13 ISBN 0 7478 0431 1.

Published in 1999 by Shire Publications Ltd, Cromwell House, Church Street, Princes Risborough, Buckinghamshire HP27 9AA, UK. (Website: www.shirebooks.co.uk)
Copyright © 1999 by Peter Wotton and Brian Oliver. First published 1999. Shire Album 347. ISBN 0 7478 0431 1. Peter Wotton and Brian Oliver are hereby identified as the authors of this work in accordance with Section 77 of the Copyright, Designs and Patents Act 1988.

Printed in Great Britain by CIT Printing Services Ltd, Press Buildings, Merlins Bridge, Haverfordwest, Pembrokeshire SA61 1XF.

This is a good-quality example of a classical marble clock with a genuine black marble case, brass bezel with bevelled glass, 'moon' style hands and white enamel dial. On the better-quality models, as in this case, the rear bezel (providing access to the clock movement) is also glazed with bevelled glass.

INTRODUCTION

The mantelpiece was the focal point of the room in any Victorian house, and amongst the impressive ornaments displayed there the centrepiece was invariably an eyecatching mantel clock, flanked by a pair of side ornaments. From the mid nineteenth century to the end of the Victorian era the most popular type of mantel clock was the mass-produced French 'marble clock'. Even though these came in a vast range of case styles and had developed from the expensive classical French clocks of the period, they tend to be instantly recognisable as a type. The stone-like case, usually black, was typically relieved with ornaments, bands and columns of coloured stone or metal, while its style was plainly inspired by the architecture of the period. These marble clocks became so popular that it was usual to find a number of them spread through the rooms of a house.

Ornaments were bought as separate items according to the taste of the purchaser. The three most popular styles were Marley horses (after a famous Paris sculpture), candlesticks and tazzas (Greek, shallow, saucer-shaped vases) such as the fine pair of classical tazzas shown.

3

Left: *Alabaster was a less expensive and very popular alternative to marble, and the clock styles tend to be much more showy. The broken pediment of this example is a form that often appears in eighteenth-century longcase clocks.*

Right: *Genuine white marble and ormolu are used in this quality clock, following a tradition going back to Louis XVI (1774–91). Clocks with an unprotected dial (not in this case), as well as an unprotected pendulum, would normally have been on a wooden base and protected by a glass dome.*

In the early years of the twentieth century the black marble cases were complemented by examples in the new styles of the Art Nouveau and Art Deco movements. These strikingly different new styles showed an original and eyecatching simplicity of line combined with the use of strongly marked and coloured marbles.

At about the same time the market became swamped with less expensive imitations, mostly, but not exclusively, from Germany and the United States. They copied the basic classical styles but also introduced new materials, wood and iron. These were so skilfully treated that, without close inspection, they are often indistinguishable from real marble cases.

4

Above: *Art Nouveau and Art Deco ornaments were offered in an incredibly varied range. This pair re-interprets the classical tazzas shown on page 3.*

Right: *This small, flat-topped marble clock in classical style is not especially striking except that the case is of painted iron and both this and the movement are American (Ansonia).*

So the term 'marble clock' can represent a wide range both in type and price. In this book, the term is taken to include any attractive stone capable of taking a high polish and also imitations in wood and metal. In 1999 a good working French example might cost around £200. In 1900 a clock of this type would have been priced around £2, at a time when £50-£100 would have been an adequate annual wage. By comparison, the more advanced marble clocks (incorporating moon phase, calendar, barometer and such like) would in 1999 cost about £1500. Clocks bought unrestored and in poor condition might be as much as 70 per cent cheaper, and sometimes even more.

THE CASEWORK

The casework of nineteenth-century marble clocks, as with other types of clock, was treated separately from the mechanism. Many retail outlets bought their clock mechanisms from one factory and the cases from another. One of the prime reasons for this was the cost of transporting the stone. By the end of the nineteenth century it was more economical to obtain stone cases from Belgium, Italy and other continental countries than from British quarries. The other continental quarries catered specially for the dominant French clock industry and were better organised to produce clock cases than their British counterparts.

The development of the marble clock case may be broadly divided into four sections: the classical phase; the Egyptian influence; the Art Nouveau and Art Deco periods; and the imitations. Though distinct in themselves, these styles overlap and intermingle. The first contains the clock styles normally envisaged when referring to marble clocks, and it should be noted that these cases were usually of slate: genuine marble was used only for the more expensive clocks.

The classical phase

The architectural forms of European public buildings during the Victorian era demonstrate the commitment to the classical Greek style. It was this grand style of architecture that became the model for so many marble clock cases and makes them immediately recognisable. The continental form of case consisted of a crude carcase covered with a veneer of black stone, and there are two aspects to consider: first, the style of the case; and, second, the method of adornment. Case styles fall into four groups: plain, drum, those with columns, and others.

Plain cases. The plain austere black case takes its basic form from the style of a seventeenth-century bracket clock with a flat top. Because this simple style was traditional it was used for some of the early, more elegant and expensive models.

A rather austere clock of excellent quality with a movement by S. Marti & Cie, one of the most popular French makers of the mid to late nineteenth century.

A smaller, unnamed and less ambitious French marble clock from the nineteenth century.

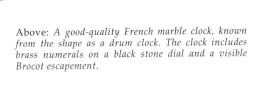

Above: *A good-quality French marble clock, known from the shape as a drum clock. The clock includes brass numerals on a black stone dial and a visible Brocot escapement.*

Left: *This drum clock is by Claude Detouche. Detouche often collaborated with the magician and automatist Robert Houdin, whose name was used by the escapologist Houdini. (Clocks by Detouche & Houdin were at the Great Exhibition of 1851.) Note the unusual, visual pendulum. This is an Ellicott pendulum, which compensates for temperature variations.*

Later variants are more ornate and show evidence of an increasingly structured approach to case manufacture.

Drum cases. The clock movement is held in a circular stone drum, which is usually supported by a pair of vertically or horizontally inclined volutes (as seen on Greek Ionic columns) and mounted on a substantial stone base. The large solid pieces of stone used in these cases both look and are heavy. To soften the effect, the surfaces were incised with sweeps of half-round fluting and inlaid with small pieces of coloured marble.

Left: *A typical French, multi-column portico-fronted marble clock from the latter part of the nineteenth century. This is a style basic to many of the public buildings built during the Victorian era. This design, with six columns, is known as 'hexastyle'.*

Right: *A typical German multi-column portico-fronted marble clock. In the more ornate examples there are two levels of column, various pediments and single figures contained in circular, tholos-styled additions. In this example the figures, known as caryatids, take the place of extra columns.*

Cases with columns. There are many variants within this grouping but three are basic.

(a) The multi-columned portico. The black cases based on the columned façade or portico (Greek, seventh to fourth centuries BC) reflect a style basic to many important public buildings of the Victorian era. In marble clocks the style dates from the latter part of the nineteenth century. The number of columns varies but six (hexastyle) or eight (octastyle) was usual. One of the more striking later variants (Hellenist, fourth to first centuries BC), particularly used for German marble clocks, exhibits two levels for the columns together with interposed figures. The use of caryatids (female figures) or canephors (figures carrying head baskets) instead of columns is also more typical of German clocks.

(b) The door-frame portico. Seventeenth-century wall and table clocks based on this form were often known as 'architectural'. It was one of the most commonly used

Left: *Classical Italian-style door-frame portico, found on many English houses of the period.*

Below: *A French door-frame portico timepiece by Farcot. Note that, for economy, the marble columns were split and glued to the black stone. The dial of this marble clock is skeletonised, with a moving frame (attached to the pendulum) mounted directly behind. Although this was a lower-priced clock, note the visible Brocot escapement using steel pallets. Jewel pallets were the norm on good French clocks.*

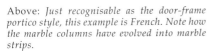

Above: *Just recognisable as the door-frame portico style, this example is French. Note how the marble columns have evolved into marble strips.*

Right: *An American example of the door-frame portico style. The connection with the multi-column portico is quite apparent; note the broken pediment.*

9

A nineteenth-century German (HAC) door-frame portico with arched top.

styles for marble clocks. There are two basic forms: the classical triangular pediment with tympanum incised is most commonly seen in French and American marble clocks (where the lines are broken at the top it is known as a broken pediment); and the arched top, particularly common in French clocks (where the arch terminates on each side with a right-angled piece it is known as a broken arch). German marble clocks more often used a crude arched top or a flat pediment surmounted by a spherical cupola. In both cases a figured brass cornice strip is common.

(c) The tholos portico. The Greek tholos (an open, circular, domed building supported on columns), like the portico, was a common architectural feature of the Victorian era. While less common in marble clocks, the tholos is usually seen expressed as two halves on either side of the mechanism housing, giving a

The larger retailers sold the case, mechanism and garniture (in this case matching) separately. The wide variations among marble clocks are here highlighted. In the black stone form, the case would be typical of a German marble clock with its domes and tholos-enclosed figures. At first sight, the bezel and clock face might suggest an American mechanism, but where are the winding holes? The attractive marble suggests that it is French. In confirmation of this, the mechanism is a French Bulle clock (an electric clock), which is twentieth-century, but it just might have been a later conversion.

10

An example of the broken-arch door-frame portico. The columns (shafts) with their top (capital) and bottom (base) 'blocks' are now only crudely implied through the shape of the curved edge. This degeneration of the architectural form is often to be seen.

distinctively different effect to the clock front.

Other cases. There is a vast range of marble clock-case styles. At first sight some appear not to fall within any classification. They are termed 'classical' because of their black stone case, finely incised gold patterns, dial and hands. Nevertheless, with close inspection it is usually possible to allocate them to the classical phase or one of the subsequent groups.

This late example of a tholos portico has only single side columns. Older examples would be black stone, with about four columns on each side and considerably more 'presence'.

The Egyptian influence

The Egyptian influence on clockmaking styles goes back to the end of the eighteenth century, when it appeared in the gilt clocks of the French Empire period (1799-1815) following Napoleon's capture of Egypt in 1798. Clocks with Egyptian figures and motifs were made during the following years and, although they are not common, they can be quite striking in appearance. In marble clocks they are usually recognisable as being related to one of the styles of the classical phase. Typically, there is a preponderance of black stone, frequently with some reference to the pyramid shape. In 1922 the discovery of the tomb of Tutankhamun caused an immediate surge of interest in things Egyptian, and this was reflected in marble clock cases. Striking decorative features are the Sphinx, Nefertiti, Cleopatra, mummies, figures and gods in the distinctive perspective of the period, hieroglyphics and pyramids.

The Art Nouveau and Art Deco phase

Three features immediately distinguish this clock-case grouping: the simplicity of the case line; the strongly marked and coloured marbles used throughout; and the distinctively different designs for the bezels, dials and hands.

Art Nouveau is generally considered to have reached its peak at the time of the Paris Universal Exhibition of 1900. The movement, British in its origins, came into its own in the latter half of the nineteenth century and remained vigorous into the early years of the twentieth century. Applied to clock cases, the new freedom was typified by a flowing, elongated continuity of line. The style

Left: While it is not immediately apparent, the vertical angle of this commonly seen style is a reference to the Egyptian pyramids. There are many other Egyptian styles, and in most cases their flamboyant markings and ornamentation instantly reveal their artistic origins.

The exaggerated sweep of the bird's wings dominates this Art Nouveau/Deco clock. Despite the difference in the case style, the movement is the same as used in classical marble clocks.

is most evident in the large ornamental figures dominating the clock cases of this period and in the flowing shapes of the oval bezels and numerals.

French in origin, Art Deco is generally assumed to have been named as a style at the Paris International Exposition of 1925. As a clock style, it is typified by designs based on geometrical figures and angular shapings. This may be seen in the clock faces characterised by the sharply angular bezels and numerals.

Art Nouveau expressed an explosive freedom from the narrow, formalised discipline of Victorian art forms. Art Deco, on the other hand, exhibited an inherent desire to return to the concept of order and structure but reflected the achievements of modern science rather than the styles of classical antiquity. These two styles are often combined to excellent effect in the marble clocks of this phase. Up to the time of writing, clocks of this group have remained highly underrated and their prices have stagnated. This seems bound to change.

Left: *Simple, almost stark in appeal, the Art Nouveau dragonfly becomes an important part of the display in this otherwise Art Deco clock.*

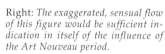
Right: *The exaggerated, sensual flow of this figure would be sufficient indication in itself of the influence of the Art Nouveau period.*

Left: *This alabaster-cased marble clock is complemented by the exquisite matching side ornaments shown on page 17.*

A clock just bought from an antique fair and ready for restoration. The black case and drum surround (mechanism removed) immediately indicate the inspiration of the French drum clock. However, with the volutes missing, there is something decidedly different about the style. In fact, it is another example from Ansonia, c.1890. It is made of iron, and its stark, clipped, no-nonsense style of decoration, so much a part of nineteenth-century America, would surely add atmosphere to the sheriff's office in a western.

The imitations

In the mid nineteenth century there was an established market for expensive, high-quality French mantel clocks. The enormous market for marble clocks depended on the aspirations of the middle classes and on their highly competitive price. This price was based on mass production (by the standards of the day, that is) of the mechanism and an equally efficient approach to case construction.

The imitators, as is usual in such situations, attempted to take a slice of the market by further substantial price reductions. Chief among these competitors were the Americans, whose techniques of mass production of mechanisms were novel and the best available. This was only a part of the package, however. Geographically separated from the economic supply of European casework, the Americans developed their own styles. The result was some original and very attractive additions to the classical case repertoire. Particularly worthy of mention are the striking styles developed by the Sessions Clock Company, whose case ornamentation, combined with painted marbling on a wooden carcase, is an art form in its own right. Unfortunately, the patina of these clocks is especially susceptible to insensitive restoration.

The more enlightened clockmakers in the Black Forest in Germany, appreciating the economic importance of the new manufacturing techniques, quickly introduced similar machinery and methods for producing the mechanisms. One of the most prolific and best-known companies was the Hamburg American Clock Company, whose logos (crossed arrows and/or the letters HAC or HAU – U for *Uhrenfabrik,* meaning 'clockmaker') are regularly to be found. The Black Forest had its own excellent traditions, and its clocks, though of recognisable origin, usually imitate case styles that follow the classical Greek tradition.

Marble clocks were made in other countries, including Great Britain, but these never achieved great popularity.

American marbled wooden clocks vary considerably in their effect. Sometimes the columns are made of blackened brass, sometimes marbled, as here. The link to the French original is apparent, but the clock is nevertheless quite distinct in style. This example is by Gilbert, a famous American company.

14

A superb example of the use of fine intaglio designs to relieve any monotony caused by the case size. The designs are Greek in origin, and the case is probably Belgian, while the clock mechanism itself is German. Even when the mechanism has not been seen, the style of the numerals, face and non-enamel chapter ring (the ring containing the numerals) gives a clue to its German origin.

Methods of adornment

As people become familiar with a new and popular product, attempts are made to retain market appeal by increasing visual impact and by implied technical innovations. Various methods of ornamentation were introduced to 'lighten' the effect of the classical black carcase: *intaglio* – finely incised patterns (using designs such as may be seen on the Greek vases in the British Museum) and channelled fluting; *relief* – small shapes and figures attached to the stone surface;

Relief ornamentation was added in a variety of ways. A popular form was a small scene in brass (often painted black) at cornice level; this example is American. Such cornice scenes are more common on American and German marble clocks.

Another example of relief ornamentation, this time French. The finely detailed figures are of brass, painted black.

15

A good example of inlay using a variety of coloured marbles and malachite. The gold work has been restored.

inlay – coloured stone inlay, classical scenes and individual figures; *columns* – according to Greek temple designs, see page 8; *top ornaments* – ornaments and figures of every shape, size and quality placed on the top of the clock case; *side ornaments* – pairs of ornaments (sold separately), on marble bases and matching the style of the clock, with subjects ranging from classical to modern.

Above: *The classical case-top ornament of this marble clock is of a shape widely used for many contemporary objects from small vases to large garden ornaments. These top ornaments are often in the form of famous figures from antiquity and literature, in which case the value of the ornament may greatly exceed the value of the clock.*

Right: *Ornaments based on Marley horses (Marley was the French sculptor of the original in Paris) were some of the most popular of the period. The quality varies enormously, with castings in bronze, brass and spelter (zinc). This excellent pair of spelter ornaments shows detail far better than average.*

The freedom of expression after the classical period encouraged every variation in style. This quite exquisite, abstract pair of side ornaments, although in a softer cheaper stone (alabaster), is nevertheless just as striking as the more ambitious sculptured ornaments of other styles. The clock that goes with them is pictured on page 13 (bottom).

Materials

Marble clocks and side ornaments were made from stone, metal and wood. The material range was limited and related to the price of the raw materials and the cost of shaping them. In the earliest clocks, even those moderately priced, exposed metal surfaces were gilded. The gilding was primarily to prevent tarnish and was later replaced by tinted, transparent varnish coatings that were cheaper, easier (done by dipping), safer (mercury gilding is lethal) and equally effective.

(a) *Stone.* Geologically, stone is classified as igneous (from volcanic action), sedimentary (from the deposition of pebbles, sand, grit, clay and similar) and metamorphic (from sedimentary rock altered through influences such as heat and pressure). The stones used for marble clock cases and ornament bases were marble and slate. By definition, true *marble* (calcium carbonate) is a metamorphic limestone, although the term is also loosely applied to non-metamorphosed limestones (Belgian *slate*). The term *limestone* is applied to any sedimentary rock consisting of carbonates: the basic constituents are calcite and dolomite. *Slate* (aluminium silicate) is a metamorphic clay. The only other stone commonly used (as a cheap alternative) was *alabaster*. The name alabaster is applied to two entirely different materials of similar appearance: hydrated calcium sulphate (sulphate of lime, the softer of the two) and calcium carbonate (carbonate of lime). In Europe sulphate is usually meant, whereas in Egypt alabaster refers to the carbonate, which was used for statuettes, bowls, vases and similar. Geologically, the material is calcite, while the massive form of calcium sulphate is known as *gypsum*. Marble effervesces on the application of acid (e.g. a drop of vinegar) while true slate and alabaster do not.

True marbles were used on the more expensive clocks. In the mid nineteenth century slate was about a third of the price of marble and was extensively used for marble clock cases, the surface being treated to imitate black marble. In very broad

17

Another pair of ornaments in the Art Nouveau/Deco style, this time recognising the vases so often used in the classical phase.

terms, any clock with more than a simple strike (chimes, date, barometer etc) is likely to be made of marble.

(b) *Metal*. The metals normally used for marble clocks were brass, iron, steel, bronze and zinc. *Brass*, an alloy of copper and zinc, was used for clock movements, gears, bezels and sometimes dials and ornaments; *iron*, for clock cases and painted ornaments; *steel*, an alloy of iron and carbon, for gear shafts, screws and hands; *bronze*, an alloy basically of copper and tin but often with some zinc, for the most expensive ornaments; and *zinc* (spelter) for the cheaper ornaments. (Note that the term 'spelter' is also used for brazing solder, which is an alloy of copper and zinc.) Bronze ornaments have the greatest value, but the prime features of any ornament are its detail and artistic quality.

Use of the term 'ormolu' often causes confusion. The French *or moulu* refers to the gold powder that was used with mercury as an amalgam. The amalgam was brushed on to the metal, and the mercury driven off by heat. The process is damaging to health and is now forbidden by law. The modern equivalent, an electro-plated finish, is not as attractive. Some consider that only bronze treated in this way should be referred to as ormolu, but brass and spelter similarly finished are often so labelled.

(c) *Wood*. The only wooden clocks considered here are those painted in a black enamel to imitate black marble. These are invariably German or American in origin and typically follow the columned classical format. The wood used is usually a soft wood of a type available in the area of manufacture.

THE MECHANISM

Marble clock mechanisms (movements) were made as simple timepieces (with only the 'going' section and without a strike) or complete with a mechanism for striking the hour on a gong or a bell (the strike section). Bells were fixed directly to the back plate of the mechanism, while gongs were separately mounted on a sounding board set into the base of the clock.

The going section consisted of: the mainspring to power the clock (contained in a barrel on French and most German clocks); the gear (wheel) train, enabling the mainspring to keep the escape wheel (the last gear in the chain) rotating for a week

Right: *The rear view of an American Ansonia clock. As with most American clocks, the springs are not restrained in a barrel. The patent mentioned at the bottom of the movement refers to Ansonia's version of the Brocot escapement.*

The mechanism of a German marble clock, unusual in that the strike is on a bell. Otherwise fairly typical, the clock was made by HAC.

19

Left: *A German movement (bottom centre) and two French movements: (left) the less common square movement; (right) the more usual round movement. In French and German clocks, mainsprings were held in a barrel (top left). The German movement uses thinner brass, was less well made and has lantern pinions.*

Right: *Anchor escapements: (left) the usual French solid anchor; (right) the usual German and American strip anchor.*

Left: *Two of the three gears of the motion work are clearly to be seen in this skeletonised dial. The canon pinion is hidden and runs inside the hour wheel; it drives the minute wheel and connects to the minute hand. The minute wheel, the lower gear, drives the hour wheel. The hour wheel, the upper gear, connects to the hour hand.*

on a few turns of the winding key; an escapement (escape wheel and anchor), with the anchor under the control of the pendulum, allowing the escape wheel to 'escape' one tooth at a time; a pendulum to control the rating of the clock through the escapement; and motion work (three extra gears just behind the dial to drive the hands).

Although a wide range of escapements has been used, only two types are usually found in marble clocks: the *anchor* escapement, which is hidden from view, in solid

The visible Brocot escapement was a very popular feature of French and American marble clocks but is rarely seen on German marble clocks. The Ansonia version is commonly seen at antique fairs. The reference to their American patent, 14th June 1881, is to be found on the back plate.

pallet (French clocks) or strip pallet form (German and American clocks); and the *Brocot* escapement, placed where it could be seen between the dial and hands. In a very few examples the Brocot escapement is placed inside the mechanism.

To work properly, a marble clock needs to be set on a level surface and positioned until the tick sounds perfectly even. If it does not, slightly loosen the two screws securing the movement, at the rear of the case, then gently twist the dial (and hence the whole movement) until the tick from the escapement sounds perfectly even. If an even-sounding tick cannot be achieved, look at the escapement anchor; heavy marks in the metal where the wheel teeth connect must be removed or the clock will cause endless trouble.

The rating (fast/slow) of a pendulum clock can be adjusted via the small nut at the base of the pendulum rod; shortening the rod makes the clock run faster. Because *in situ* adjustment would be rather impractical on a heavy mantel clock, most marble clocks have an accessible shaft at the top of the dial marked F/S or A/R (fast/slow or *avance/retard*). This effectively shortens the rod from the top of the pendulum. French clocks use either the Brocot or Vallet adjustable pendulum suspensions. German and American clocks are different, vary considerably and are sometimes quite novel: occasionally, this feature is missing completely. F/S shaft adjustment is via a small, double-ended key, as used on carriage clocks and early anniversary clocks (those

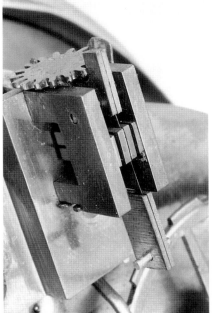

The most common French suspension block is the Brocot version. The pendulum hangs from the spigot piercing the brass strips (bottom right). Turning the shaft at the top front of the dial (with the small key) turns the toothed wheel (top left). Via an attached threaded rod (hidden), the toothed wheel raises or lowers a block (centre of picture), clamping the suspension spring (clamped at the bottom by the brass strips). Movement of the block effectively allows a fine control over the length of the pendulum rod. German and American methods are much more variable and sometimes quite ingenious.

Temperature compensation for the metal pendulum rod was achieved in marble clocks either by mercury tubes or by the Ellicott system. Mercury, held in two tubes and with freedom for upward movement, was used to compensate for the downward movement of the pendulum bob with increase in temperature. The example shown is an American imitation on which mercury-filled glass tubes are replaced with shiny metal tubes merely for display.

with disc pendulums).

Marble clock mechanisms were usually accurate and, though they can be affected by problems such as hardening of the oil, they were not oversensitive to changes in temperature. There was, therefore, little benefit to be gained from a temperature-compensating pendulum. However, the extra interest gained by the use (in French clocks) of a visible Brocot escapement and a visible, moving pendulum was further enhanced when the pendulum was constructed from mercury-filled glass tubes or the expanding rods in the Ellicott system. One manufacturer, Farcot, offered a skeletonised dial with a moving shape behind it (attached to the pendulum).

Above left: The temperature-compensating Ellicott pendulum was first devised in 1732, and the one used in marble clocks is much the same. Downward movement of the pendulum rods (outer rods) operates the lever that raises the pendulum bob in compensation. This pendulum is peculiar to French clocks.

Above right: In a French marble clock the count wheel is always on the back plate of the mechanism and is easily seen through the rear door of the clock; the rod from left to top centre of the picture is for striking the bell. A French rack and pinion strike would be on the front plate and be hidden by the dial. German and American striking systems are less easily distinguished without removing the mechanism from the case.

Solid pinions (French, top) and lantern pinions (German and American, below). There is a long tradition of lantern pinions in German and American clocks, while French clocks invariably used solid pinions, which are considered superior.

Farcot is also particularly known for its 'cherub-on-a-swing' (Gautier escapement) clocks in an alabaster case.

Marble clock strike systems appear in two forms: count wheel, and rack and pinion. The difference in the two types is easily distinguished visually and may best be seen from the illustrations. The count wheel (or locking plate) is the older system but was cheaper to produce, and so it was still being used into the twentieth century (for example on the French Art Nouveau/Deco clocks). Practically, the difference is noticed only when re-setting the hands. With the rack and pinion system, the number struck corrects automatically to the time displayed by the hour hand. With the count wheel system, the strike can come out of step. In the latter case there is sometimes a rod provided (accessed through the back of the clock – not on French marble clocks) to operate until the number of strikes is in agreement with the hour hand. Alternatively, turn the minute hand to the hour, allowing the clock to strike; turn the minute hand anti-clockwise (just past the click – about five minutes to the hour); turn the minute hand to the hour and allow to strike; repeat the process until the hands and strike are synchronised.

The typical French movement was of outstanding quality. While there are exceptions (for example, the work of Seth Thomas of the USA), German and American mechanisms were usually of appreciably lower quality. In general this would mean thinner brass, lantern pinions, inferior dials and poorer form and registration of the gear teeth. Too much should not be read into this, however. The imitation marble clocks that are most frequently to be seen at antique shops and fairs (for example HAC from Germany and Gilbert and Ansonia from the USA) were differently constructed. Properly restored, such mechanisms last as well and can be just as accurate as their French counterparts.

Around 1900 a German mechanism without strike would have cost about ten shillings and with strike about seventeen shillings. A French mechanism would have cost twice as much in each case. French mechanisms were offered for both seven-day and fourteen-day operation between windings. The main advantage of the latter was the more constant spring force, giving better timekeeping over a seven-day winding period.

A basic stone case for a French movement under 30 cm wide with two gilt columns would have cost about £2 in 1900. Imitation cases were hugely variable and competed with the most popular clocks of the day. An equivalent German imitation marble case (painted wood) would have cost about five shillings. Cases, particularly later, were retailed with a choice of different types and makes of movement, which would have been installed at the time of purchase.

COLLECTING AND RESTORATION

One of the most attractive aspects of collecting is buying a bargain; another is the satisfaction of turning a filthy broken wreck into a valuable working antique.

First check the nationality of the manufacturer. As a rough guide, French clocks have winding holes close together, round movement, fleur-de-lis shaped hands, and a circular glass rear door (on more expensive clocks). American clocks have widely spaced winding holes, large gears and rectangular movement, stylised fleur-de-lis shaped hands, and coarser design. German clocks have more widely spaced winding holes, large round movement with thinner plates, hands similar in shape to American ones, domed cases and figures within or in place of columns. German and American clocks mostly use lantern pinions.

Next examine the case. Dirt is unimportant, but the type of damage is critical. Go through the following list carefully, noting the condition of black stoneware, coloured stoneware, imitation stoneware, ornamentation, dial, bezel, glass, hands and, if present, visible escapement. Try and make a rough estimate of the cost of professional repair. A coded indication is given here as a guide to the approximate cost of professional work. This is on a scale of 1 to 5, with 3 representing a price around that paid for the clock. For suitable experts try *Yellow Pages* and *Clocks* magazine.

Black stoneware (3–5+) can be invisibly repaired by a good stonemason. Serious damage to coloured stoneware (5+) will usually reduce the value of the clock to that of its parts only. Imitation stoneware (2–3), wood or metal, is reasonably easy to repair. All damage to ornamentation (1–3 as reasonable) is repairable – even to the

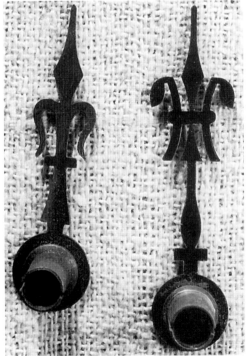

re-casting of an ornament. A number of companies offer dial (3+) restoration. A bezel (2–3), if seriously damaged, may have to be repaired rather than replaced: this is straightforward but requires skill. Glass (1–2) replacement, even if it has to be bevelled and fitted, presents no problems. Missing hands (1) and missing visible escapement jewels (1–2) are easily replaced. The cost of a complete professional overhaul in 1999 (cleaning, oiling and adjustment) would be about £100.

If at all possible, check the mechanism. Look at the visible tips of the winding shafts: heavily pitted rust and damage to the squared edges are danger signs and easily seen. As long

Clock hands appear in many styles. The fleur-de-lis version is the one most commonly seen on marble clocks. The French (left) and American (right) interpretations for the hour hand are distinctly different and offer an immediate, quick confirmation of the country of origin. German hour hands tend to follow the American style.

24

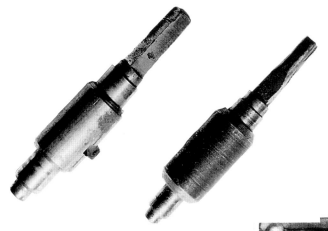

Left: *The condition of the winding square indicates how the clock has been treated. Heavy rust and broken edges to the square are visible from the front of the clock without disassembly. Note that surface rust is easily removed, but severe, pitted rust may mean that an expensive repair will be required.*

Right: *A wooden board at the bottom of a marble clock acts as a fixing point for a gong as well as improving the sound. Note the outer slate layer covering a crude, light-coloured carcase.*

as rust on the steelwork (in particular the gear shafts) is light, heavy untouched dirt all over is encouraging. All parts of the mechanism are repairable, but at a price. Find out whether a replacement mechanism has been fitted, indicated by a poorly fitting dial or bezel. A missing pendulum is easily replaced, as are the connections on which it swings. Check whether the clock will tick. Be aware that a common trick is to soak the mechanism in oil to make it go (which is almost useless) and sell it as 'working'. Note that, if allowed to harden, the deposits from over-oiling can be difficult to remove.

Restoration

After disconnecting the pendulum and bell, or possibly a gong (screwed into the sounding board below), start by removing the two screws at the back of the clock. Gently pull out the mechanism from the front and put it to one side. The following description outlines a restoration level that is mainly assessment plus a few simple techniques easily used by the untrained. More detailed techniques and sources for the materials mentioned may be found in books and articles listed under 'Further reading'.

Casework. If the case is in reasonable condition, do no more than polish it. Use a pure, non-tinted beeswax. Black grate polish is also effective, particularly if there are faded patches visible on the surface.

Be very careful when lifting the case, because the cement holding the pieces together is often weak and easily becomes softened with damp and age. For this reason, washing in water is not usually recommended, but if the case is very dirty it is the most effective first stage (except for alabaster, for which white spirit should be used). Use warm water with plenty of washing-up liquid and a touch of disinfectant; work quickly, rubbing hard with a dryish sponge; work on small sections of the case at a time. The case should be tilted sharply so that any free liquid drains rapidly. 'Jif' and 'Flash' can be used for stubborn deposits (not on true marble). Rinse thoroughly but rapidly, and dry

Left: *Remove the two screws at the back (one is shown removed in the photograph), making sure that the movement is supported from the front as this is done. As was common, the back of this slate clock has been left unfinished, as can be seen from the discolouration and poor appearance of the slate still in its original condition.*

Below: *This slate base is in poor, faded condition and is shown after washing down. The good black-coloured area round the hole has been protected by the clock. At the front, three sections are visible, separated by tape: the left-hand section has been left untreated; the centre section has been waxed with an unstained pure beeswax; the right-hand section has been treated with black grate polish only. For best results finish with wax.*

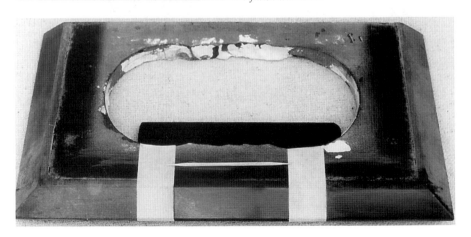

off immediately with a paper towel. Complete the process with a hair-dryer.

Within limits, small pieces of broken stone can be replaced by cut-offs from old clock cases. If you do it yourself, use a piercing saw (with a blade for cutting metal) wiped with beeswax. Coloured stone can be imitated almost imperceptibly with home-made scagliola (and some skill).

Most cases will be slate. In the mid nineteenth century slate was finished to imitate marble by japanning (the European version, not Urushi). This would have meant the application of a spirit-based varnish – French polish pigmented with lamp-black. By the end of the nineteenth century slate was advertised as enamelled: for the amateur, Aspinall's 'Ebonica' (c.1890), offering a 'jet brilliant black', was a typical cold-cure enamel. Up to the early years of the twentieth century this meant a pigmented, oil-based (linseed) varnish that dried to a high gloss. At that time varnish was a very broad term for a resin (the list used was large) in a spirit or oil base. Aspinall's enamel was probably an oil-based varnish with a high proportion of resin (for the gloss) pigmented with asphaltum. Note that asphaltum is easily degraded by coal fires and sunlight.

Where the stone is badly discoloured, first sandpaper (fine and wet); then apply slate blacking (a special dye from horological suppliers) to darken the surface; then polish with beeswax to finish. Black grate polish is a quick and very effective alternative. Lastly, to bring out the gold intaglio, first wax the whole clock; scratch out the design with a pointed cocktail stick; rub an antique gold wax crayon heavily across the design, and remove the excess with a feather edge (a cocktail stick sliced with a fine-bladed craft knife is ideal); then polish hard to finish. Alternatively apply gold paint with a very fine brush.

One simple way to restore the gold work (as in a number of examples in this book). Clean out the pattern with the point of a cocktail stick. Using a good-quality gold wax crayon, rub hard over the pattern (upper part of picture). Slice the cocktail stick to a long feathered edge (as in picture) and skim across the slate, leaving only the gold in the pattern. Rub hard with a strong paper towel (lower part of picture). An untinted wax polish can then be applied across the whole surface if needed. Restoring the gold work should be the final stage of the restoration.

This example shows a paper dial (German) imitating one of the more expensive enamel dials. Where such a dial is badly damaged, first disassemble it. Photocopy the pieces, paint out any damage using typists' white correction fluid, then re-photocopy. Age the photocopy using a diluted (methylated spirit) French polish, testing first. Cover with plastic film (such as that used for book protection), then reassemble.

Dial. Attending to the dial is a little more ambitious. Remove the pin securing the hands and the three pins behind the front plate holding the dial assembly in place. The hands and dial assembly should be easily removable. The dial will usually be one of three types: silvered metal, paper or enamel. For silvered metal dials silvering kits work well and are easy to use. With a paper dial, as a last resort photocopy the disassembled pieces, age or tint the paper with French polish heavily diluted in methylated spirits and cover with plastic film. For an enamel dial, if damaged down to the copper, fill with white porous filler, scrape to slightly below dial level, tint with watercolour, and cover with transparent nail polish.

Metalwork. Work will probably be limited to cleaning brass bezels, for which something like Brasso will be perfectly adequate. Use Brasso well beyond the 'black' state. Be aware that the bezel would have been gold-plated and any remaining plating will be removed by such harsh abrasives. When it is clean, wipe well with methylated spirit and apply a coat or two of French polish with a soft paper kitchen towel. With a little experience an excellent finish can be achieved without leaving application marks or towel residue.

MAKERS, MARKINGS AND LOGOS

Clock mechanisms are covered with small marks that may identify the retailer and give details about the mechanism, the maker and the date. In addition, inside the case there may still be old paper labels or notes giving further details of the purchaser, the retailer or the price, or even delightful period ephemera.

Names on the enamel dial are usually those of the retailer unless the maker is particularly well known. Added names do not have the durability of the original markings and tend to be removed by cleaning.

The makers whose marks are most commonly found on back plates are: from France, S. Marti, Japy Frères, Vincenti; from Germany, Hamburg American Clock Company (HAC), Philip Haas, Junghans, Badische; from the USA, Gilbert, Ansonia. (See 'Further reading' for sources of lists.)

Nearly all marble clocks have a serial number on the back of the mechanism, and some include the maker's logo. Be aware, though, that the larger intermediaries often had their own name added instead of that of the maker. Information is patchy, but for the better-known companies this may be of use when attempting to date the clock.

Most marble clocks include a number indicating the length of the pendulum in inches (from the suspension point to the centre of the bob). Note that one French

Marks on the back plate of the mechanism can be of great interest. In this French mechanism can be seen the serial number (bottom left); the length of the pendulum, 4.8 French inches (i.e. 5.12 imperial inches, bottom right); the logo of Japy Frères, mentioning their Medal of Honour. They were awarded a number of medals. This logo is c.1888.

29

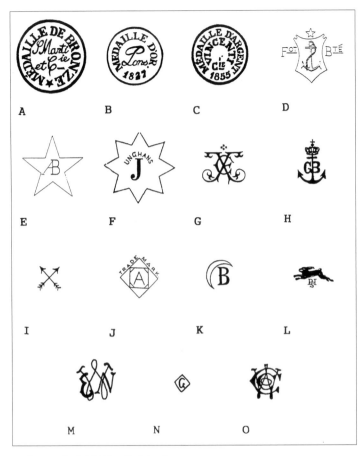

This is a selection of the more common logos to be found on the back plates of marble clocks. They are not the only logos used by these companies. For further details see K. Kochman, 'Clock and Watch Trademark Index' (1982).
A, S. Marti & Cie; B, Honore Pons; C, Vincenti & Cie; D, Farcot; E, Achille Brocot; F, Junghans; G, Japy Frères & Cie; H, Gustav Becker; I, Hamburg American Clock Co (HAC) or Hamburg Amerikanische Uhrenfabrik (HAU); J, Ansonia Clock Co; K, Badische Uhrenfabrik; L, Phillipp Haas & Soehne; M, E. N. Welch & Co; N, William L. Gilbert Clock Co; O, Waterbury Clock Co.

inch equals 1.066 English inches.

Regular exhibitions throughout the nineteenth century offered medals of various types. Logos and replicas of these, with the dates, are often to be seen on the back plate.

A range of initials such as DRP (Deutsche Reich Patent – German Empire patent) may also be present. The German patent office is very helpful and some of the patents are fascinating to research (see D. K. Stevenson, 'German Patent Letter Clues', *Clocks*, volume 21).

Repairers often leave repair dates and data hidden behind the dial on the front plate.

Marks, punched dots and small cuts are to be seen on the mainspring barrels, one mark for the going, two for the strike. Later repairers often added a G and an S.

Other markings, such as bin number, team (clocks were assembled by small teams) and even setting-up marks (for example, the strike wheels), can be found by stripping the mechanism. Such marks are usually not much help in the history or dating.

FURTHER READING

Many of the most interesting specialist books and articles are old, long out of print and difficult to obtain. Specialist booksellers, whose advertisements appear in *Clocks* magazine, may be able to supply back numbers of that journal as well as the books in the second list that are marked with an asterisk*. The other books listed should be more generally available.

Articles in *Clocks* magazine
Aked, Charles K. 'A Matter of Suspense', volume 9, 10, pages 21-4 (1987).
Bartlam, J. N. 'A Well Travelled Japy', volume 11, 10, pages 52-3 (1989).
Bartlam, J. N. 'Magic Numbers', volume 18, 2, pages 23-4 (1995).
Bartlam, J. N. 'Brocot Calendar Regulators', volume 16, 8, pages 28-30 (1994).
Bartlam, J. N. 'Marvels in Marble', volume 14, 2, pages 21-3 (1991).
Bartlam, J. N. 'What Medals', volume 20, 13, pages 17-18 (1997).
Bernbrock, John. 'Repairing Black Marble Cases', volume 18, 6, pages 9-12 (1995).
Hobden, Mervyn. 'Polishing Marble', volume 1, 10, page 19 (1979).
Jackman, D. H. 'Flea Market Folly', volume 11, 11, pages 14-18 (1989).
Jackman, D. H. 'Monster of Marble and Brass' (three parts), volume 17, 4, page 51; volume 17, 5, pages 44-6; volume 17, 6, pages 42-3 (1994).
Jackman, D. H. 'Black Marble White Elephant', volume 11, 6, pages 19-22 (1988).
Jackman, D. H. 'A Modest Bargain' (two parts), volume 14, 7, pages 12-15 (1991); volume 14, 8, pages 32-6 (1992).
Jago, T. C. 'A Black Marble from Birmingham', volume 16, 7, pages 26-30 (1993).
Page, Roy. 'Breathing New Life', volume 20, 2, pages 26-9 (1997).
Page, Roy. 'Restoring Enamelled Wood Cases', volume 20, 8, pages 18-21 (1997).
Penman, Laurie. 'Dating Your Marbles', volume 6, 9, pages 19-21 (1984).
Pickering, Clive. 'A Cast Iron Clock', volume 16, 1, pages 46-9 (1993).
Powell, Edward. 'Hidden Treasure', volume 17, 12, pages 16-19 (1995).
Stevenson, D. K. 'German Patent Letter Clues' (two parts), volume 21, 4, page 32; volume 21, 6, page 39 (1998).
Tyler, E. J. 'Clocks Cased in Iron', volume 7, 6, pages 25-6 (1984).
Wallage, Peter. 'French III', volume 1, 4, pages 42-5 (1978).
Wilford, Alf. 'Striking Americans', volume 14, 7, pages 28-31 (1991).

Books
Adams, Carol (compiler). *Guide to the Antique Shops of Britain*. Antique Collectors' Club, twenty-eighth edition, 1999-2000.
*Davies, D. C. *Slate and Slate Quarrying*. Crosby Lockwood & Co, 1887.
de Carle, D. *Practical Clock Repairing*. NAG Press, 1982.
de Carle, D. *Watch and Clock Encyclopaedia*. NAG Press, 1983.
*Doussy, Michel. *Antiques: Professional Secrets for the Amateur*. Souvenir Press, 1971.
Erhardt, Roy. *Official Price Guide to Antique Clocks*. House of Collectables (PO Box 149, Westminster, Maryland 21157), third edition 1985; regularly updated.
Johnson, Lorraine. *How to Restore and Repair Practically Everything*. Michael Joseph, 1984.
*Jones, Bernard E. (editor). *The Amateur Mechanic*, volume III. Waverley Book Co, c.1900. (For scagliola.)
Kochman, K. *Clock and Watch Trademark Index*. Antique Clocks Publishing, Concord, USA, 1982.
*Lawrance, James. *Painting from A to Z*. Sutherland Publishing Co, 1938.
Shenton, Alan and Rita. *Collectable Clocks 1840-1940*. Antique Collectors' Club, 1996.
*Stalker, John, and Parker, George. *Treatise of Japanning and Varnishing*. Alec Tiranti Ltd, 1998 (originally published 1668).
Thorpe, Nicholas M. *The French Marble Clock*. NAG Press, 1990.
Williams, Merfyn. *The Slate Industry*. Shire, reprinted 1998.
*Young, Dennis (editor). *Repairing and Restoring Antiques*. Ward Lock, 1979 (republished by Peerage Books by arrangement with Cameron Books Ltd).

PLACES TO VISIT

Marble clocks were in vogue from the mid nineteenth century to the 1930s, when their popularity went into sharp decline. Since the 1980s, when interest in collecting began, there has been a steady rise in value and interest. However, museum clock collections have concentrated in other areas. The London museums have excellent clock collections. The Wallace Collection is the best for French clocks; these are from an earlier period but give an idea of the foundations on which the marble clock market was built.

Attingham Park, Shrewsbury, Shropshire SY4 4TP. Telephone: 01743 709203. Eighteenth- and nineteenth-century English and French clocks.
Science Museum, Exhibition Road, South Kensington, London SW7 2DD. Telephone: 020 7938 8000. Website: www.nmsi.ac.uk
Victoria and Albert Museum, Cromwell Road, South Kensington, London SW7 2RL. Telephone: 020 7942 2000. Website: www.vam.ac.uk
The Wallace Collection, Hertford House, Manchester Square, London W1M 6BN. Telephone: 020 7563 9500. Website: www.the-wallace-collection.org.uk

The best places to see a good range of marble clocks and to gain experience and access to specialist knowledge, as well as the opportunity to purchase, are antique shops, antique fairs and horological fairs. Antique shops are listed in *Guide to the Antique Shops of Great Britain*, published by the Antique Collectors' Club.

Antique fairs are advertised in local newspapers and may also be listed in *Antiques Info Magazine*. In Great Britain the major shows are those now organised by DMG (Daily Mail Group), of which the largest are at the Newark and Nottinghamshire Showground and at the South of England Showground, Ardingly, West Sussex.

Major horological fairs, the largest of which is held at Brunel University, Uxbridge, Middlesex, are advertised in *Clocks* magazine (website: members.aol.com/clocksmag/homepage.htm).